TESTIMONIALS

Sound strategies, fiscal responsibility, and marketing well are all important for a successful business. But Peterman Brothers has put genuine and meaningful empowerment for every member of the team as the top priority. They've become one of the fastest growth and well-beloved organizations in America, and Chad will humbly deliver the simple yet effective secret to that success that will transform your organization.

—Jonathan Bancroft
President, Morris-Jenkins
Author, Mr. Jenkins Told Me...Forgotten Principles That Will Grow Any Business

The Empowerment Project by Chad Peterman is a compelling read that resonates with my experiences as a fellow business owner in the industry. Chad's story highlights his experience of growing Peterman Brothers by putting his employees first while emphasizing that creating and maintaining a positive work culture is an ongoing process that requires intentional effort and long-term commitment. If you're a fellow service industry business owner struggling with growth and positive culture this is a great read for you!

—Aaron Gaynor
Owner and CEO, Eco Plumbers, Electricians, and HVAC Technicians
GetEco.com

T0266532

Chad Peterman has earned the nickname "Perfect Chad" for a reason. The challenges of making partnerships work, particularly when succeeding one's own father in a family business, are expansive.

I attribute his humility, kindness, and capacity for learning and application as key factors in his achievements. Together with his brother, they have propelled the Peterman brand to new heights, without sacrificing the culture, morals, or quality that define their family's business.

I wholeheartedly endorse this book for anyone who may find themselves navigating similar circumstances. For those who inherit their family's business, Chad's insights offer invaluable guidance on the path to excellence. And for fathers approaching retirement, Chad's father's perspective challenges conventional thinking and is a testament to embracing the transition of leadership.

—Travis Ringe
ProSkill Services

This book, *The Empowerment Project*, is a masterclass in transformative leadership. It is now clear to me how Chad Peterman has built one of the fastest growing admirable businesses in the home service industry. From cultivating future managers to handling trust issues, each section is a strategic blueprint for building empowering cultures and high-performing teams. Through real-world case studies, Chad navigates industry pitfalls, offering invaluable insights for executives and managers seeking to drive organizational success. This book is a must-read, providing practical strategies for fostering growth, enhancing communication, and creating dynamic workplaces. Chad's people-centric approach is a game-changer for those shaping vibrant, innovative teams. Backed by Gallup insights, he emphasizes the importance of prioritizing employees' well-being, both personally and professionally, setting the stage for a guide that is not just about business success but also about creating positive, inclusive cultures that drive sustained organizational achievement. Each page is a testimonial to Chad's commitment to fostering continuous improvement and putting employees first. A resounding "Great Job!" to Chad and his dynamic team!

—Ken Goodrich
Founder and Chairman, Goettl Home Services

Luck is when preparation meets opportunity, and this is a perfect playbook on how to create your own luck both professionally and personally. Chad shares a number of successful tactics to help you be prepared by showing that if you genuinely care, trust, and push yourself and others to constantly be better, you can and will win!

—Chris Yano
CEO, RYNO Strategic Solutions
Host, To the Point Home Services Podcast
RYNOss.com

The Empowerment Project encapsulates the heart of our family business. It beautifully emphasizes that fostering personal growth within our team is as vital as their professional development. This book embodies the essence of valuing people, enriching both our company culture and the lives of our employees. Highly impactful!

—Trey McWilliams
CEO
Blue Cardinal Home Services Group

There is always much to be learned from an individual that is vulnerable enough to share their challenges as well as their victories. I applaud Chad for writing this book to educate and empower others through his story. Read this with a notepad to capture your ideas as you will find yourself inspired and empowered as you read Chad's story.

—Julian Scadden
President, CEO
Nexstar Network

THE
EMPOWERMENT PROJECT

THE
EMPOWERMENT PROJECT

GROW YOUR PEOPLE, GROW YOUR BUSINESS

CHAD PETERMAN

Published by Advantage Books, Charleston, South Carolina.
An imprint of Advantage Media.

ADVANTAGE is a registered trademark, and the Advantage colophon is a trademark of Advantage Media Group, Inc.

Printed in the United States of America.

10 9 8 7 6 5 4 3 2 1

ISBN: 978-1-64225-862-2 (Paperback)
ISBN: 978-1-64225-861-5 (eBook)

Library of Congress Control Number: 2023924698

Cover design by Matthew Morse.
Layout design by Ruthie Wood.

This publication is designed to provide accurate and authoritative information in regard to the subject matter covered. It is sold with the understanding that the publisher is not engaged in rendering legal, accounting, or other professional services. If legal advice or other expert assistance is required, the services of a competent professional person should be sought.

Advantage Books is an imprint of Advantage Media Group. Advantage Media helps busy entrepreneurs, CEOs, and leaders write and publish a book to grow their business and become the authority in their field. Advantage authors comprise an exclusive community of industry professionals, idea-makers, and thought leaders. For more information go to **advantagemedia.com**.

CONTENTS

CHAPTER 6

Delivering the Skills: Top Tech 49

CHAPTER 7

Prioritize Recruitment 55

CHAPTER 8

Sharing Empowers Everyone 61

CHAPTER 9

INTRODUCTION

In 1986, my father took a leap that would change his life—and mine—forever.

Money was tight, but he went ahead and started Peterman Heating & Cooling in Beech Grove, Indiana, with just one truck and a garage. He had a simple philosophy: provide great service to one home at a time, truly caring about that family and the work that needed to be done.

When I joined the company in 2011, it had revenues of $1 million from residential heating, ventilation, and air conditioning (HVAC) work in central Indiana and twenty-one employees who were experts in their specialties. They could handle any HVAC issue known to man. They talked about heating the same way a car guru talks about the intricacies of an engine. Each of them brought a special skill and passion to the table.

Then there was me.

I had a passion for making the business better, but I was green, and I had none of the specialized, high-level knowledge the experts had.

My dad, who was gradually preparing for his well-earned retirement, had a unique approach for me. Instead of holding me back, he unleashed me. Sure, he added guidance here and there, but his philosophy on handling his naïve-but-enthusiastic son's ideas was this: never say no.

No matter how bold (or bad) my ideas were, my father encouraged them. Things didn't "click" overnight. Every lesson was hard-fought and hard-earned. But after a decade, my father's approach paid off, even with my many mistakes.

One of my ideas for growing the company was one you don't often hear from business executives: empowering employees. Following that guideline, my brother and I took charge of the company in 2015—now named Peterman Brothers—and grew it to over six hundred team members and revenues of over $100 million in eight years.

I credit my father. Actually, I credit his examples of empowering others—from the technician on the front lines, to the field manager, to upper-level management—which helped the company perform at its best.

Many people in our industry believe good front-line workers are hard to find, hard to train, and harder to keep; however, we feel they're not only worth the effort, but they're our number-one asset, as well. Yes, even above our customers. We empower them by freeing them up to have new ideas and act on them, and we all reap the benefits.

From one truck and a man with a dream, Peterman Brothers is now one of Indiana's prominent residential plumbing, heating, air conditioning, and electrical services providers.

I'm writing this book to tell you about the key to our phenomenal growth: *empowering our employees.*

CHAPTER 1

CULTURE IS A VERB

Many business owners trying to scale their companies obsess over marketing strategies and targeting the right customers, but in my experience, the best way to grow a business is to focus on the most important "customers"—the company's employees.

If the only goal is to make money, a business is going to struggle. Our main goal is to empower our people so that they can be successful and fulfilled in their work.

A company's culture—the way it approaches day-to-day business and how it treats employees—is very important. Workers need to know they're in a safe place where they can make a mistake now and then, and they won't be punished for it; they'll have the chance to grow from it.

When a company's culture empowers employees by training them for leadership roles—teaching them the day-to-day skills they need to become great managers—a business runs well and scales quickly, and team members know they're valued parts of the enterprise.

An Empowering Culture

In our company, culture is a verb—an action word.

To empower employees, a company needs a positive, supportive culture, and that kind of culture doesn't just happen. Many companies think it simply comes from a leader's personality—they don't see it as something that needs to be developed.

A great corporate culture comes from an intentional internal process, the result of many efforts within a company, and those efforts are never finished.

Many times, when a company doesn't have this type of culture, people are so fearful of making a mistake or a poor decision that they're paralyzed—they don't act at all.

I agree with clergyman and author Norman Vincent Peale: "Action is a great restorer and builder of confidence. Inaction is not only the result, but the cause of fear."

When you put your people first and empower them, they gain the confidence to take action without fear.

Peterman Principle

Followers think of themselves first; leaders think of others.

Paradigm Shift

In the home services industry, the dreaded phrase that repair technicians hate to hear is "on-call." Most companies designate one technician as on-call for a week at a time—that person works full days and then takes service calls after hours. When our company used the on-call system, technicians often logged ninety hours a week.

A conversation with Chris Hoffman, President and CEO of Hoffman Brothers in St. Louis, Missouri, gave me a new perspective on this. He said, "At our company, we don't have on-call."

"How does that work?" I asked.

"Our people come first," he said. "When someone is exhausted from working eighty or ninety hours in a week, what kind of service are they going to give to the customer? And that person's family life is going to suffer—how would your marriage be if you were away from home all that time?"

"I'm sure it wouldn't be great," I said.

"Last year, we made this shift and decided that if a customer calls at a late hour, we're going to answer the phone," he said, "but instead of making our tired on-call person respond right away, we tell them we'll be there first thing in the morning."

At that moment, I realized that our company can't claim to be about empowering employees while we make some of them work way too many hours, which might damage their health and surely affects their family life.

We made the paradigm shift for the good of our service technicians. These days, we tell customers who call at all hours of the night that they'll have to wait until the next day for service because our people come first. Our technician will be there first thing in the morning.

We still have team members who choose to work long shifts to pick up extra hours, but they're never required to work a ridiculous number of on-call hours. This is part of employee empowerment—showing our people that we want them to have a positive experience at work as well as enough free time to enjoy their personal lives.

Spreading Positivity

I believe in empowering through positivity. As the leader of our company, I'm the catalyst for our culture. The way that I act can be contagious—it tends to be how our team members act and how they treat one another.

Setting a positive tone empowers employees by giving them energy and an optimistic outlook. Without question, these things boost productivity, help our employees stay engaged in their work, and enhance their relationships with one another.

I'm an introvert by nature, but a while ago, I realized that to be an effective leader and to scale the company, I was going to have to be an extrovert to a degree. So every day when I walk into the office, I say hello to as many people as possible and ask them how they're doing. I want our team to know I'm in a good mood and ready to have a great day. You don't need a special talent to do this—you just have to make the effort.

Some of our people come from companies where the leaders yell and scream, but the last thing I want is for our people to be afraid of me. In the eleven years that I've led Peterman Brothers, I haven't raised my voice to anyone, not even once. I want people to remember that I'm just another part of the team, and our business wouldn't be as successful without all of us respecting one another and pushing in the same direction.

To let our team know we're moving forward, I send out an email every Monday morning to remind them we can accomplish anything if we put our minds to it. Here's an example:

The most powerful weapon you have at your disposal is your mindset. If you think you can't do something, you're right. If you think you can do something, you're right. We hold the key to our results in our minds. We have the power to learn from any and all things that happen. Never allow anyone or anything to change your mindset. Wake up early and prepare to tackle the day, knowing that you're going to serve others and learn, regardless of the outcome. Will you be easily shaken or know that you are in control? Obstacles aren't problems; they're opportunities to get better. Go be great today in the face of what is going on in our crazy world. We own our success.

In our main lobby, we have a library of leadership books for our people to read. We announce monthly "Acts of Greatness" that recognize those on our team who are going above and beyond. These are just a few of the ways in which we empower our people with messages of positivity that help them stay engaged in their work, boost their productivity, and achieve their goals.

Peterman Principle

Go chase the impossible and discover your potential.

Personal Empowerment

I regularly encourage one-on-one meetings with every member of our team. Meetings with the entire group serve a purpose, but the most meaningful connection happens when I sit down with someone individually and try to understand where they're struggling and how I can help.

These meetings are an essential part of a supportive, empowering culture because they let every employee know they're important to me and our company—they deserve focused, individual attention.

In a company such as ours that is growing so quickly, the pace is very fast, and our people must handle many different tasks. In many instances, meeting with someone who is struggling and working on their time management will show them that, while they're very busy, they're devoting too much time to the wrong tasks. They need to focus their efforts on tasks that are essential for achieving the results we're looking for.

Often, these conversations lead to a direct, tangible form of empowerment: training. We continually invest in training programs that prepare our team for growth and their next role in the company.

We have more than fifty team members enrolled in our Leadership Academy, which gives them leadership training that is customized for our industry. In 2022, with the help of our training programs, we were able to promote 15 percent of our team to higher-level positions.

Another way that I empower our people is called Future Leaders. It's not really a training session; I just talk for an hour on a specific leadership topic (e.g., our team's efforts to create their own "Five Steps to Personal Growth" plan). To make sure there's a steady flow of these talks, I do them every other Friday, and the following Monday morning I send out an email to ask if anyone has questions. This gets our week off to a positive start.

Many Decision-Makers

In the trades, many owners started out as technicians, and because of their high skill level, they believe "no one can do it as well as I can." When they move into management, that attitude can persist, making them want to make every decision themselves.

An essential way to empower employees is to get them involved in decision-making. If the leader of a business is the only person making decisions, that company is going to have a very slow growth trajectory because of the time it takes for that one person to address every issue. The pace of operations can slow to a snail's pace and frustrate employees who need to move quickly.

I had the "blessing" of not starting out as a skilled technician— I didn't think I knew it all—so it was easier for me to distribute decision-making to many other people.

When our business was in its early days and my brother and I were much younger, our dad told us he made all the big decisions, but to scale his business, he had to accept the fact that he couldn't do everything himself—he had to coach and support his people so that they could make decisions on their own.

If someone asks me to make a decision they're capable of making, I say, "I trust you to make that decision. I hired you because you're an expert in this and I'm not, so you make the call. I'm confident great things are going to happen."

When we empower people by giving them authority, it creates a positive energy in our culture that many employees haven't experienced before. It's like a light bulb flashes and they think, "This is so different from the last company I worked at. Since you trust me to make this decision, I'm going to make the right one and make the situation better than before because it's mine. I own a piece of our success as opposed to just clocking in and clocking out, making money for the owner."

When someone asks me, "How did your company grow so much?" I answer that we have a ton of awesome people with many different skill sets all rowing the boat in the same direction.

Peterman Principle

People follow those whom they believe care
about them and have a plan.

Develop Future Managers

Companies make the mistake of never training people who work on the front lines to be managers. I always tell our technicians, "If you're going to lead people, I need you to trade in your tool belt with the tools you use to fix a furnace, and put on your leadership tool belt because you're no longer the technician, you're the one who develops the people on your team."

Helping employees get those skills is critically important—the more people you have ready to lead, the faster you can scale your business.

In three short years, one of our employees went from being a service plumber, to managing a department, to leading an entire branch. For me to see that person's progress, their satisfaction from what they've accomplished and the excitement they feel about learning new things are the most rewarding parts of owning my business. It reinforces the fact that our positive, empowering culture works.

Show Your Gratitude

Years ago, a mentor of mine taught me the importance of writing handwritten thank-you notes to employees. This is part of the empowering culture, letting people know we care about them.

Some leaders say, "I don't have time to write thank-you notes; I have more important things to do." I say if you don't have time to thank your people, you won't get the results you're looking for because they won't feel invested in your business.

I have a goal to write two thousand thank-you notes this year. It's the right thing to do for your people, and it's the right thing for your business.

Empowering our employees is one reason why Peterman Brothers is making an impact in this world. To me, that's far more important than saying we're the biggest company. I always say our goal is to grow better, and growing bigger will take care of itself.

A common roadblock that stands in the way of empowering employees is business leaders who can't let go of "doing things my way."

Case Study: Crystal Valley Comfort

Four years ago, Sheila Barczak was hired as an operations manager of Crystal Valley Comfort, a family-owned heating and cooling company in Elkhart, Indiana, to make the company as profitable as possible before the owner sold it and went into retirement.

The owner was leaning toward selling the firm to an established business in Indiana, but after Sheila met with that company's leadership team, something didn't feel quite right.

"I sat down with their board of five people, and they repeatedly questioned me about myself and our company—I felt they were interrogating me and I felt disrespected," Sheila said. "They said they had never been in the HVAC space before, and I know it's a business you have to have a deep knowledge of and truly understand. After a brief discussion, they said they had to cut our meeting short to prepare for another one. They abruptly got up and left. I was totally turned off because their culture seemed uncaring and impersonal."

During this time, Sheila was learning more about Peterman Brothers. She decided to listen to a podcast Chad did and was impressed by how much focus Chad poured into his people and how he wants to impact his employees' lives for the better and make a difference in the community. She decided to give Chad a call as a potential buyer for Crystal Valley.

"I found out we're aligned in how we want our companies to be run," Sheila said. "Chad invited me to visit Peterman Brothers headquarters and one of their branches to find out what it's like to become a Peterman company. I had never been offered that opportunity before—clearly, he wanted to display the company's culture, and that gave me a positive feeling."

Sheila and two managers from Crystal Valley went to a Peterman location in Indiana, and the visit was the first step in Crystal Valley becoming a Peterman Brothers company.

"From the moment you walk into Peterman, you feel that it's a warm, friendly culture," Sheila said. "Chad met us personally and gave us a tour of the entire building. As we walked, he knew every employee's name. We saw the training facility and he described how the company tries to make the most out of every employee's ability and create leaders. My dream for Crystal Valley is to develop a culture that will make it the best place to work in northern Indiana. I'm confident that, as a Peterman company, we will realize that dream."

Next, I explain why it's so important to hand over the keys to the leaders in an organization and let them benefit from the company's trust.

CHAPTER 2

STOP DOING AND START TRUSTING

During my time in business school, none of the textbooks mentioned a principle that we've followed for years at Peterman Brothers: *trust your employees.*

Giving employees your trust—we show our people trust from the moment they start with us—achieves a few important things. First, it helps them feel good about themselves—they realize we have confidence in them to make sound decisions. If workers don't feel that a company will support their decisions, they won't make any.

Trusting employees helps a business function efficiently because workers won't ask their manager what they should do—they go ahead and make the decision themselves. This saves a ton of time.

A leader who trusts their employees realizes that their role isn't to solve problems, but it's to remove roadblocks so that their team members can solve them. This is an area where a lot of managers limit their department's growth. Their team realizes it's OK to bring a problem to the leader and that person will solve it. Because of that, the team doesn't perform as efficiently as it should and their department doesn't scale.

As an organization becomes bigger, there are hundreds of decisions to be made every day, and if many of them aren't made, the company won't move forward.

Peterman Principle

Opportunity finds those who seek it in every situation.

Ask the Right Questions

As the owner of my company, people often look to me for answers, but I tell them, "You don't want my opinion—my opinion might be terrible because I don't have technical experience. I'm a leader, not a technician. I don't know how to do your job—that's why you're here."

Often, in a meeting with an employee, I'll say, "I understand that's the problem—what would you do to solve it?" This allows that person to be creative in coming up with a solution and gives them ownership of that solution—it empowers them.

Recently, we did a huge inventory and procurement project. It took seven months to complete, involved thirty-five of our people, and benefited our company greatly. I didn't attend one of the many meetings for that project—I had zero input into the outcome. I just handed the project off to our director of continuous improvement. She assembled the team, and they ran with it. I entrusted the team to get it done, and done well, and they did exactly that.

If a leader is fortunate enough to find great people and add them to their team, trust and empowerment must be there, or they won't get much done. I'm comfortable knowing what I'm good at and what

I'm not, and for the things I'm not good at, I find great people who are, and I trust them to do their thing.

Hire People Who Are Smarter Than You

One thing that shows a manager has the ability to trust is when they hire people who are smarter or more skilled than they are. A manager must have the self-confidence to do that because that's when everyone feels free to use their strengths to the fullest.

Peterman Principle

On his tombstone, the industrialist Andrew Carnegie has this inscription: "Here lies a man who knew to enlist people better than himself."

When a leader hires experts, they create something much stronger than a company—they create a culture in which people feel empowered and trusted for their high level of skills.

Handle Trust Issues

I always tell people who want to be managers that their biggest hurdle might be overcoming a trust problem. You can't scale a department from two technicians to one hundred if you micromanage the people on your team or if you don't trust them to do the things you need them to do.

Here's a five-step process that we use for helping our managers overcome their reluctance to trust:

- *Trust first* – Our managers give employees trust from their first day on the job. When a decision has to be made, trust that an employee will make a good one, and give them the freedom to make it.

- *Demonstrate* – If a team member is having trouble making a decision, the manager should show them how they'd like it to be done. This will help them move forward by giving them a model to follow for future decisions.

- *Recap* – Meet with the employee one-on-one, and make sure they understand all the key points in making a decision.

- *Allow them to do it and remove obstacles* – When a decision has to be made, stay out of the way, and let the employee make it. Remove anything that could be an obstacle to a clear decision.

- *Improve* – After the decision is made, talk with the employee about what went well and what could have been done better.

Peterman Principle

Leadership is stewardship—service above self-interest.

Don't Try to Fix People

A mentor of mine once said, "Everybody is perfect just the way they are."

If that is true, then as a leader, it's essential to connect with them on their level. Some people are hands-on; some like to see a bullet list of key points; some are more visual and prefer colorful graphics.

It's a manager's job to find out the best way to make that connection and give the employee help based on what works for them. It's essential to meet that person where they can learn and grow.

Case Study: The Level of Trust Affects Morale

When a leader micromanages employees—insisting on being involved in every detail of their work—it stifles empowerment and individual growth.

Deb Albacete, director of continuous improvement at Peterman Brothers, shares her point of view:

In my career, I've witnessed micromanagement and its impact. Generally, leaders have the best intentions, thinking they're protecting their team by being "deep in the weeds" with them, ensuring everyone is on track with minimal room for error. What they don't understand is that, even though they want to help, this does the opposite of empowering employees—it makes them feel that there is a lack of trust in their capabilities. The goal should always be to foster a trusting work culture which inspires confidence in employees and gives them room to grow and develop on their own.

Kurt Conner, director of human resources at Peterman Brothers, had experienced a lack of trust in the opposite way. In a previous job at a national company with seven hundred employees, his bosses didn't micromanage everything he did; they barely made contact with him and his colleagues on the front lines.

Kurt said:

Our management team—my direct manager and his supervisor— didn't have a presence at the work site, so they didn't speak to employees or listen to us about changes we'd like to make to improve performance. We had a lot of great ideas, but they wouldn't meet with us—they held meetings only with high-level managers and the things they said trickled down to the rest of us. When they made changes, they wouldn't tell us why. I wanted to be very involved in the business, but I felt frustrated because I was totally disconnected with what the company was doing.

When Kurt joined Peterman Brothers, he learned in the first week that the company would trust him because management wanted employees to make decisions, make mistakes, and get out of their comfort zone and learn.

These days, Kurt passes that trust on to others:

The hardest thing when it comes to delegation and trust is when you're passionate about something you did well—who can do it better than yourself? But in keeping with the culture at Peterman Brothers, I put total trust in the rest of my team, and they feel empowered by that. People feel free to make decisions on their own, knowing they won't be punished for a mistake; it will be seen as an opportunity to learn.

In addition to trusting employees, leaders can empower them by putting them first. Most companies put all their focus on their customers, which seems to make sense, but in doing so, they often alienate their most important asset—their employees.

CHAPTER 3
PUT EMPLOYEES FIRST

One of our top sales managers at Peterman Brothers, TJ Shackelford, came from companies that had very different cultures than ours, cultures that didn't value employees' time or their personal lives. I'll let him tell his story:

Nearly every other employer I had didn't value me as a person—all they focused on was, "This is the job and these are the things that we need to do. Get it done!" In my previous job, I was finance director at an automobile dealership. The company had a lot of great employees, but many times, I was swamped and I had to work for entire weekends. One of those times, I had folders for fifty finance deals on my desk and I didn't know how I would get through all of them.

I finished the work and decided to take the next day off. At home, I was sitting on the sofa when my eighteen-year-old daughter came down the stairs and said, "Hey Dad, what are you doing?"

"I'm just taking some time off," I said. "I'm exhausted and I need to recharge."

"OK, I'm surprised to see you because you're never home," she said as she left the room.

The way she said that really dug into my heart. It pained me to realize that I need my job to provide for my family, but I was working so much that I was missing my kids' entire lives. I was making a big mistake working seventy hours a week and I didn't want it to continue.

That's what brought me to Peterman Brothers. I love the company's culture and how they value the time employees spend with their families. The company eliminated the need for employees to be on-call and make service calls at all hours of the night. Our office staff just schedules those repairs for the next day.

I'm not required to work on Saturdays. On many Saturdays, my wife and I wake up and cook breakfast together. After breakfast, we grab our two youngest kids and go see a movie matinee, have some lunch, do a little shopping, and come home. In all my previous jobs, I wouldn't have been able to do that. I missed all those wonderful moments with my family. That's something that Peterman Brothers has enabled me to have.

A while back, I sent a text to Chad thanking him and Peterman Brothers for giving me forty-three Saturdays in a row with my family. It's been many more than that now, and I'm grateful.

Peterman Principle

It's one thing to set your potential; it's another thing to truly believe you can achieve it.

Training Comes First

The times when someone teaches us something—how to solve a math problem, how to become better at a sport, how to cook a great meal—help us not only by giving us new skills but also by making us feel we're worth teaching. That person knows we have the ability to become better.

That's why training and developing our employees are at the forefront of what we do. We put our people first by setting them up for success. Nothing makes us happier than helping someone grow their skill set so that we can give them a higher position as well as a higher paycheck.

In our business, a large part of training is actually retraining. When a new employee comes from a company that wasn't focused on developing them, they often have mediocre skills and a negative outlook on their future. We train that person to let them know we're putting them first by helping them enhance their careers. We let them know they're worth it!

On the business side, we develop our people because when the labor they provide is better, we can sell our services at a higher price and pay our team more.

It's been shown that training enhances workers' morale on the job and their loyalty to the company. When someone believes their company offers excellent training opportunities, they're less likely to leave within one year than employees at places with poor training.[1]

Having well-trained employees reduces costs as employee turnover is expensive because of time spent in exit interviews, administrative functions for termination, severance pay, and unemployment compensation.[2]

---

1   Jerry Shaw, "Effects of training on employee performance, " Chron,

    https://smallbusiness.chron.com/effects-training-employee-performance-39737.html.

2   Ibid.

Peterman Principle

Discipline yourself to see the opportunities in all situations.

Help People Improve

An important aspect of putting employees first is understanding where they're at in their skills. It's the job of our leaders to find out the quality of the skill set a person has and how they're responding to training.

Most of the time, if someone isn't getting better, it's not that they don't understand training—the leader must look inside themselves and figure out a better way to set up that person for success.

Unfortunately, there are always people who don't want help—they don't want to improve. If someone is just not accepting training, we want them to leave the business. When there are many people who are learning and looking to get better and one person who isn't, it can damage the company's culture. It doesn't take us long to spot that—most of our staff turnover happens within the first ninety days of employment.

To be honest, our culture isn't for everybody. We need people who have the mindset of "I want to keep getting better, all the time" because we're going to challenge them to improve. If an employee wants to make more money at Peterman Brothers, they have to show us that they're worth more. It's not about sticking around for years, never improving and just taking a paycheck. We need our people to continue to provide better service for our customers, and this is as much the responsibility of our leaders—including me—as our employees. We all have to work together to make sure we're always improving.

If an employee is having trouble getting the job done, it's up to their manager to say, "You're struggling—we can both see that. What can I do to help you perform better? I want you to succeed." When a leader looks an employee in the eye and says that, the employee is usually motivated to learn and work hard to raise their performance. It shows that we care about them; we want to put them first and make an investment in their career.

Peterman Principle

Leaders must provide a place where people can be at their best and create something that has never been seen before.

Make It Personal

A Gallup poll showed that, even when workplaces offered benefits such as flex time and work-from-home opportunities, employees valued their own well-being above and beyond anything else, even material benefits.[3] A key piece of putting employees first is having a culture that respects their personal lives. It's not about putting our people first only in the workplace; it's the same in a personal setting.

---

3   Emma Seppala and Kim Cameron, "Proof that positive work cultures are more productive," Harvard Business Review, https://hbr.org/2015/12/proof-that-positive-work-cultures-are-more-productive#.

For example, if an employee says she has to go home in the middle of the day and take care of her kids, that's fine—being a good mom comes first. If a dad wants to attend his son's baseball game and he has to leave work a little early, by all means, do it. We want our people to have the freedom to be the best parents, wives, or husbands they can be.

An important part of putting employees first is caring about the day-to-day environment they work in. I firmly believe that if you don't hear people talking, laughing, and having a good time in the workplace, that company isn't nearly as productive as it could be. Part of a leader's job is to curate the kind of culture in which people take their work seriously but keep a positive, enthusiastic attitude.

You'll never see me in the office without a smile on my face, saying hello to everyone I see and trying to help people. If the leader of a company is in a good mood, then everyone else tends to be cheerful too. Everyone at Peterman Brothers should be aware that our six hundred employees are doing great things—because we are—and there's no problem we can't solve.

As our employees solve more complex problems and gain a stronger understanding of our business, they're ready to move up to leadership positions. Read on to find out why cultivating leaders is one of our favorite—and one of the most important—things that we do at Peterman Brothers.

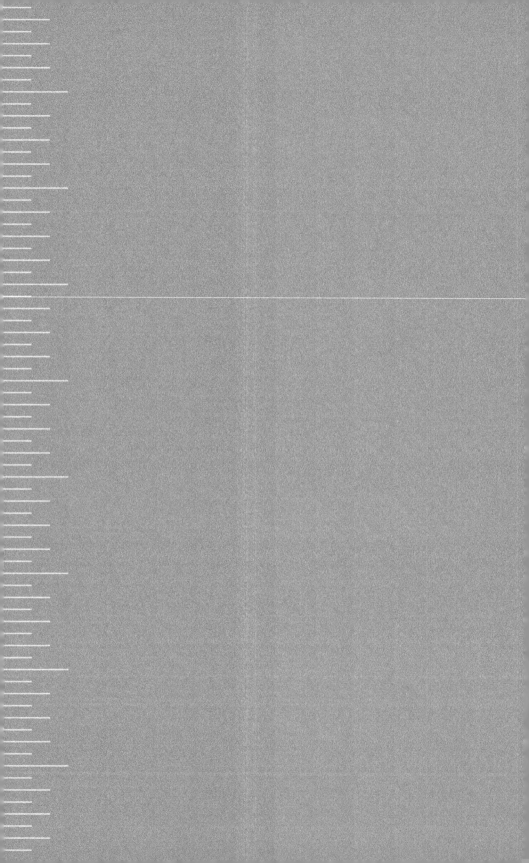

CHAPTER 4

CULTIVATE LEADERS

I'm the leader of a successful, growing multimillion-dollar company, and I can't remember the last time I made a business decision.

I make virtually no decisions—I empower and entrust my team to make nearly all of them. I'll offer ideas, but I'll support someone if they think they have a better way. I never tell people how to do their job—I want them to figure it out on their own.

Getting Out of the Way

In 2021, I got out of the operations aspect of the business. I needed to be a better leader. Instead of supporting my team and removing obstacles that stood in their way, I was trying to do too many things myself—that's easy to do in a small business where everyone wears a bunch of different hats.

When I got out of the way of leaders who were passionate about operations, our company exploded, growing more than it had ever grown before. It was a direct result of me letting people do what they're very good at.

We always try to cultivate leaders in our company. Often, owners of small businesses want to be involved in every decision, and they just can't. If there's one thing that will prevent a business from scaling, it's having one person involved in every decision.

If you're in every meeting and if you're the only one talking, you need to change that by letting your people make decisions—by empowering them.

Move Up and Lose Power

Many people in our industry—as a matter of fact, in all industries—think that when someone moves up a rung on the corporate ladder, they gain more power, but actually, they give up power. At that higher level, they might have more influence over people—either positively or negatively—but the real power rests with those whom they lead.

At that higher level, they don't do the technical work anymore. In our company, for example, they're no longer in the role of master plumber or top HVAC tech. They're in a supporting role, helping all the technicians. At that level, a leader's main job should be to remove roadblocks so that their team can accomplish great things.

It's imperative that leaders understand this. In my position of CEO, I could tell people to do something my way, but refraining from taking power allows you to build something greater than yourself.

To be a good leader, focus on providing support. Some support comes in the form of coaching. Some comes from holding people accountable. Some involves being creative and coming up with new ideas that will help your people be successful.

Leaders Must Lead Themselves

In many cases, good leaders take the initiative and lead themselves. A great example of this is Antonio Agresta, an HVAC service technician at Peterman Brothers. He spent years in the military and was an emergency medical technician (EMT) for six years after that. He was looking for a change from the high-stress world of emergency services, and he enrolled in a trade school conducted by Peterman Brothers, not only to learn a trade but also to put himself on a path to greater well-being:

I don't like being complacent—I like to become comfortable with being uncomfortable and challenging myself. I'm always striving to learn as much as I possibly can, in my personal life as well as my professional life. Peterman Brothers showed me how to become a good leader not only by learning to do a great job diagnosing HVAC systems, but also by having integrity, caring about customers and their needs so they trust that we're always going to provide great service.

Peterman Principle

Optimism, positivity, and belief are a leader's
most valuable weapons.

It Takes Confidence

When I look at leaders who are successful and compare them with those who aren't, one of the big reasons is confidence. To me, confidence is a kind of superpower because it's something that people can easily see. If someone in a leadership position doesn't have confidence, it's difficult for their team to believe in them.

Confidence breeds something that is important for good leadership—urgency. In our business, a leader has to have urgency—you have to want to make things happen right away. If a leader is too analytical and takes too much time to figure things out, their team is going to become impatient and want to move ahead without them.

Seeing the next move before it actually happens is critically important because the team will think, "OK, she's thinking a few steps ahead—I'll follow her leadership."

The most important things in building confidence in team members are giving them clear directives—telling them, "This is what you need to focus on"—and using key performance indicators (KPIs) to give them tangible evidence that they're being successful. Building confidence isn't always just patting someone on the back and telling them they're doing a good job, but it's also providing a scoreboard that proves they're winning.

A Positive Outlook

When it comes to being a great leader, optimism is very important. If a leader is pessimistic—always looking for things to go wrong—guess what? Everyone else is going to look for what's wrong and reasons why things won't work. Any time someone brings up a new idea, a pessimistic leader will provide five reasons why it can't be done.

Peterman Brothers has been in business for thirty-six years; we've tried many different approaches to our business and always found ways to make good things happen. You have to start from an optimistic position—"This could be a great idea!"—because often, an idea can get things rolling and the fine-tuning comes later.

I honestly think that if I were hired by an organization where I knew nothing about their business, if I displayed confidence, urgency, and optimism, I would be a good leader for that business. It's simply a mindset.

Looking for Leaders

One thing I do to find potential leaders in our company is listen to conversations. I listen to their manager talk about their work and how they interact with colleagues. I join group chats to see how that person responds to others. I gather this information, and if I conclude that the person could be a good leader, I just have to figure out the best place in the company for them.

This is not an exact science. Sometimes we predict that someone will be a stellar leader, and it just doesn't work out that way.

Whenever we have a leader who doesn't make it—they take a different role in our company or leave the business altogether—we always ask ourselves what we could have done better or differently. As a business is scaling and things are moving very fast, it's possible to put someone in a position where their skill set isn't right for the job or they're in over their head from the beginning. We always step back and accept some of the blame, and then we find the best place for that person and set up the next potential leader for success.

Peterman Principle

Someone who takes ownership is someone
people want to follow.

Learning to Lead

One very helpful resource for aspiring leaders is the Peterman Leadership Academy, which we started in 2019. The Academy is a resource where people who want to grow can improve themselves. There are usually about forty people in the program at a given time. They do it all on their own, and they do it outside of their work time.

People go through the training at their own pace—typically, they complete it in six months or less—and to "graduate," they must complete five levels that correspond to the rooms in a house:

- *Level 1: The Basement* – This wellness challenge requires getting an annual physical exam, kicking a bad habit or taking a daily walk.

- *Level 2: The Living Room* – Taking this financial challenge requires starting a monthly budget, opening a 401(k) account, or checking their credit report.

- *Level 3: The Bedroom* – Philanthropy is at the heart of this challenge—doing volunteer work, organizing a charity drive, or donating money to a worthy cause.

- *Level 4: The Bathroom* – Accepting this leadership challenge involves hosting a "lunch and learn" event on a business topic or working with a manager to develop a new standard operating procedure.

- *Level 5: The Office* – For this communications challenge, prospective leaders must lead a team-building exercise, plan a lunch with co-workers, or reach out to a colleague they haven't spoken to in a long time.

Peterman Principle

Great Leaders lead people, not budgets, projects, or goals.

Jarryd Stefanik is a video marketing coordinator at Peterman Brothers. He finished the Academy program in four months: "It definitely helped to shift my mindset toward what it takes to be a leader. One of the big things the Leadership Academy did was to challenge me to interact more with my team and to give credit to the people who are helping me be successful. That's very important for making the transition from contributor to leader."

Tom Shriver, HR manager at Peterman Brothers, appreciates our investment in him: "The training helped me realize that the company cares about me and my development as person as well as a leader. A lot of what we do in the Academy focuses on professional development, but there's also an element of personal development attached to each phase. It's not only about me as a professional, but as a complete person and the things I'm able to contribute to society."

Our business isn't about furnaces. It isn't about water heaters. It isn't about sales. It's about creating a place where employees are empowered, where they can become better leaders and better people. If you have an organization full of great leaders, you literally won't be able to stop the company from scaling.

It's very important, however, to give everyone in a company—many of whom aren't interested in leadership—a career path that allows them to grow. In the next chapter, I'll talk about the guidelines we follow in our hiring process—they might surprise you.

CHAPTER 5

HIRE FOR VALUES; TEACH SKILLS

You'd think that when a successful HVAC company like ours hires someone to be a technician on the front lines, we'd hire the best of the best, someone with years of experience and high-level skills. But actually, the opposite is true—we make a point of hiring people with no skills at all.

One reason is because it can be very difficult for someone who has years of experience as a plumber, for example, to "unlearn" their way of doing things—including their bad habits—and learn to do things the Peterman way. I remember a plumber we hired years ago who had many years on the job—he knew how to do every plumbing job imaginable—and he struggled for a long time to do it our way.

He specialized in doing installations, and he was very good at it. We wanted him to have a bright future with us, but he constantly created friction with our servicepeople, the ones who sold our services to customers. As far as he was concerned, that team never did anything right, and he didn't hesitate to blame them when something went wrong.

I had to do something to get him to go along with the program. I set up a few one-on-one conversations to empower him by letting him know there was a place for him at Peterman Brothers, we valued his skills and experience, and we wanted him to stay with us.

It took some time, but my message finally clicked with him. He said he understood that to fit into our culture, he had to change, and the change he made was remarkable. He tried hard to work as part of the team, not as someone who was constantly critical of his colleagues.

He's now our plumbing service manager, leading a multimillion-dollar-a-month department. He regularly participates in our leadership training programs and has total buy-in from the plumbers on his team.

A few years ago, when our Top Tech Academy reached the point where it offered training in everything for heating, cooling, plumbing, and electrical, I realized we could teach anyone all the skills they need, and it was best to focus on hiring people with three personal qualities—we won't compromise on this: *they had to be hungry, humble, and smart.*

Peterman Principle

Be a force in your life; don't just wait for things to happen.

In his book, *The Ideal Team Player*, Patrick Lencioni lays out his formula for hiring based on these three values. In an interview with *Forbes* magazine, Lencioni talks about this: "The kind of people that all teams need are people who are humble, hungry and smart. Humble being little ego; focusing more on their teammates than on themselves. Hungry, meaning they have a strong work ethic, are determined to get things done and contribute any way they can. Smart, meaning not intellectually smart but inner personally smart."

They understand the dynamics of a group of people and how to say and do things and have a positive outcome on those around them. The way to find these kinds of people is to be very intentional in interviews about those qualities and to understand that those qualities are more important than technical skills.[4]

The All-Important Interview

An important factor in finding the right people is our interview process—asking the right questions.

To explore whether a prospective employee is *hungry*, we ask questions about their ambition, such as the following:

- Describe a project or idea that was implemented mainly because of your efforts. What was your role, and what was the outcome?

- Tell me about a situation in your past that demonstrates your willingness to work hard.

- What projects have you started on your own? What prompted you to get started on them?

When we try to find out if a job candidate is *humble*, we ask interpersonal questions such as the following:

- Tell me about a time when you had a conflict with another employee or customer. What caused the conflict, and what steps did you take to alleviate the problem?

4 Dan Schawbel, "3 Indispensable virtues that make teams successful," Forbes.com, https://www.forbes.com/sites/danschawbel/2016/04/26/patrick-lencioni-3-indispensable-virtues-that-make-teams-successful/.

- Describe a time when you had to communicate negative information to a supervisor or customer. How did you give them this information, and what was the result?

- What qualifications for this position do you lack? Please describe what you need to do to compensate for that.

Here are a couple of questions to find out if a prospective employee is *smart*:

- Describe a complex situation in which you had to comprehend a lot of information quickly. How did you go about learning the information, and how successful was the outcome?

- Describe a time when you came up with a creative solution/ idea to a problem in your past work.

In some cases, an interviewer will look for something very specific. Dan Bates, plumbing service manager at Peterman Brothers, explains:

For an installer, one of the things I look for is someone who doesn't get flustered easily. That person can go out there with customers, keep a level head and understand that he has the ability to do this and not let the task break his spirit and drag him into a negative mindset. They're someone I could send out to a job that isn't going well, and when he arrives on the job everybody thinks, "Oh good, he's here."

When someone exhibits qualities like this, it's good to know that we can invest in this person and investing in them will be good for everyone involved. I get the distinct feeling that this person isn't just going to fill a role, but they're also going to help with the growth of Peterman Brothers.

When we interview somebody and we know they're a good fit for our company, my mind doesn't think of what they will become on day thirty or day ninety; it's what they will become years from now and how big a part of this company can they be.

Peterman Principle

Always ask: How am I developing myself, and how am I developing others?

Abundant Opportunities

Since our company is always growing, we're always creating job opportunities, and not all of them are leadership positions. Someone wants to be a leader or not. Everyone at Peterman can follow a long, satisfying career path without ever taking a leadership role. For example, a technician can move from level one to levels two, three, and four—we provide the training they need to reach every level of expertise. They can keep moving up within one department if that works best for them.

When employees want to talk with managers about their career path, managers have to know how to communicate effectively with them.

Managing Dreams

A critical part of building empowerment is helping employees understand the connection between work and their personal goals and dreams. We've found that if the two aren't connected, an employee has less incentive to work hard and improve their performance.

For example, if someone on our team has the dream of buying a house for their family, we want to know that so that we can ask ourselves, "How can we help them get there?" We communicate to the person what their performance needs to look like—what they need to learn and how they need to improve—to earn enough money to afford that house.

We never approach this type of improvement as, "We want you to do better so you make more money and Peterman Brothers does better." We see it as, "We want you to do better so you and your family can take that trip to Europe you've been dreaming about." Then we figure out the steps involved in achieving that.

Another aspect of helping people realize their dreams is finding the job that fits them the best. Jeremy Curtis, branch manager, describes one such person:

An employee went through the Top Tech program, worked in plumbing maintenance for a while, but he found his way to our training department. In his life before Peterman, he was a teacher and enjoyed that work. We had an opportunity in that department, we worked to get him onto that team, and it suits him very well. He's not in a leadership position, but because there's so much opportunity at Peterman, he was able to find his passion and he loves what he does on a daily basis.

Peterman Principle

Find discomfort; allow yourself to go to the edge; you need to be scared!

Everyone Is a Leader

In some way, shape, or form, we're all leading. It's not about the difference between finding people who want to be leaders and people who don't. It's getting everybody in the organization to recognize that they're leading from their own position, whether it's an apprentice technician or someone managing an entire branch. When they realize they're leaders, the rest will take care of itself.

Recently I was in a classroom where we graduated ten new plumbing students. Back when the plumbing instructor was a technician, if I would have asked him, "Do you want to be a leader?" he'd probably say, "No, I'm a plumber. That's what I know how to do." But I can tell you for sure that all ten of those students appreciated the huge impact he made on their lives. He didn't stand in front of the class giving a leadership speech; he's leading through his willingness to help others.

Kristy Muse, operations manager at our company, gives her perspective:

We're constantly preaching that it doesn't matter what role you have at Peterman, we're all a leader in some capacity. Some people don't have confidence in their skills, so as we coach them and show them what we see as their abilities, it builds their confidence. They just need someone to believe in them and let them make decisions on their own. The path we lead them down is that they have to make mistakes and learn from them—they can't let mistakes hold them back.

We focus on finding great people, with the goal of teaching them all the skills they need, but exactly how do we teach those skills? We don't send them to trade schools or recommend online courses—we have our own school right here at Peterman Brothers.

CHAPTER 6

DELIVERING THE SKILLS: TOP TECH

Back in May 2020, when Dad was nearing his retirement, he put an old office building that Peterman Brothers wasn't using anymore up for sale.

I had the idea to create our own school that would train workers in our way of doing things, and I needed a place to put it. I went inside the empty, worn-out building, and as I walked around, I envisioned classrooms where the old offices were; a few conference rooms could become hands-on training areas. Those spaces were ideal for teaching our people the skills they needed.

I left the building—my initial, sketchy plans for the school fresh in my mind—and I called Dad.

"I'm sitting in my car in front of the old building and there's a big For Sale sign here," I said. "I have an idea to start our own school so we can train our people the right way, and I think we're going to need this building to put it in."

A long pause. "Chad, I just got a good offer on the building, so I intend to sell it," he said. "I thought we were a heating and plumbing company, not a school."

I asked, "Can you tell the buyer that you changed your mind and you're not going to sell? We'll rent the building from you so we can start this school. What do you think?"

After another pause, he said, "I've always told you to value your ideas and pursue them with all your heart, so I think you should pursue this one."

Dad took the building off the market, and we began building our school there. We called it Top Tech.

Peterman Principle

Growth is the only way to ensure that tomorrow is going to be better.

Labor Shortage

Qualified technicians in the skilled trades are very hard to come by. For Peterman Brothers, Top Tech started out as a way to train people and combat the labor shortage at the same time. Our company was growing very fast—we had more customers than we had workers to service them—and we couldn't find enough technicians fast enough to keep pace.

Alan Richardson, HVAC instructor at Top Tech, sees it this way: "A lot of skilled technicians are retiring, and there aren't enough people going into the field to make up for it. A main reason for this is the longstanding belief that to be considered successful and to support a family, you have to go to college for four years. And the HVAC trade, which can be lucrative, is not a four-year-degree type of thing."

The Top Tech program has a curriculum like any school, with courses, semesters, grading metrics, and graduations.

The education is structured based on the specific services we provide for our customers. For our servicepeople in HVAC, electrical, and plumbing, training programs are eight to ten weeks long. Since the people we hire have little or no background in the trades, we start them from ground zero, and when I say ground zero, I really mean it: "This is a wrench. Here's how you use a hammer. This is the right way to roll up a hose after you use it."

During those weeks, we provide a solid foundation through classroom learning, hands-on training, and going out on customer calls with experienced technicians.

After three months of that, we determine whom the top performers in a class are, and they move on to three additional levels of training. If they're successful, they qualify as full-fledged service technicians, and they can go on calls on their own.

The program for our HVAC installers has similar steps, and in about ten months, an employee can go from having no technical skills to being a lead installer with their own truck and, possibly, an entire career ahead of them.

Brandon DeBlaso, who progressed quickly from HVAC technician to call-by-call coach during his time at Peterman Brothers, was a member of the first Top Tech class in 2020. He describes the experience this way:

When you start, it's a bit overwhelming, just like the first day of school, and I was nervous as I began to learn this new trade. When I got home, I said to my wife, "I wonder what I've gotten myself into." But the next day, Chad got up in front of our group and said, "What we do isn't rocket science; it's just learning how to fix furnaces and air conditioners. The most important thing we teach you is how to give world-class service to our customers." That reassured me that Top Tech would help me succeed by giving me all the skills I needed, not just for the technical side, but for the people side as well.

Peterman Principle

Work your plan each day, with the understanding that you are headed where most people are unwilling to go.

Focused Instruction

With Top Tech, the pace to get to senior-level positions is much faster than other methods because of the concentrated training the program provides. In the past, technicians could take five years to learn all these things, but they never had anyone training them—they were just going through the motions out in the field.

We guide someone through classroom teaching and time spent in the lab working with tools to fix mechanical problems, but just as important, each student knows we're giving them a career path and plenty of opportunity within Peterman Brothers and elsewhere.

For each year's Top Tech class, we get more than two thousand applications from people wanting to attend. That tells us two things: There's a lot of interest in the training that Top Tech provides—some people call it the "Harvard of Trade Schools"—and there are few good trade schools left.

Building a Workforce

How will we in the trades continue to get good people? We're going to have to "build" them on our own. Sorry to get on my soapbox, but we need to stop complaining about the lack of a workforce and build it, because it isn't coming from anywhere else.

Peterman Principle

Your ambition must be stronger than all obstacles.

When technicians receive Top Tech training and they know how to fix any mechanical problem that comes their way, they can shift their focus to the business we're really in: people.

Drew Gomez, plumbing instructor at Top Tech, explains: "I've been at Peterman for ten years and I'm a thirty-five-year veteran of the plumbing trade. It's important that the technicians we train care about what they do, but even more important, they have to care about our customers. We can teach them all the technical skills they need, but we can't teach them to be genuine and empathetic about a customer's situation."

Our director of training and development, Andrew Hasty, feels that teaching our technicians to improve their people skills gives them a valuable foundation for the future:

When we give someone the tools they need—not just the hard technical skills, but also the art and science of communication—those are skills that set people up to be successful in whatever career they choose. Whether they want to continue into the trade they've chosen or change to a completely different type of work, these are intangibles they can leverage to develop their professional acumen, but just as important, their ability to connect as a human being. We're teaching transformational skills, and that's the really empowering part of Top Tech.

I've observed firsthand the fact that Top Tech provides so much more than technical skills. I've sat at graduation ceremonies of our "students" and nearly had tears in my eyes listening to them talk about how the training has given them a career, a way to provide for their families and, for many, a way to fulfill their dreams.

The journey to all those great benefits starts with recruiting, the first step in the challenging process of bringing great people to Peterman Brothers. It's the most important part of our entire business.

CHAPTER 7

PRIORITIZE RECRUITMENT

Some departments at Peterman Brothers are visible as they do their work—service, training, and installation are a few. But one group that usually operates behind the scenes is the "engine" that makes our entire company go: recruitment.

We're in the business of selling skilled labor, and the only way for our company to grow is to recruit more of that labor. It's all about increasing capacity—if you can do more work in a day, you can do more in a month and in a year, and your company reaps the rewards.

A fast, efficient recruiting process reduces costs, boosts our reputation, and makes sure the most skilled workers are identified, attracted, and brought into our business.[5]

The Challenges of Recruiting

For many companies in our industry, recruiting seems difficult, but that's because they don't give it a high priority. They don't have anyone in the role of recruiter actively searching for great people. They think,

---

5   Tanya Ridding, "The Importance of effective recruitment, LinkedIn, https://www. linkedin.com/pulse/importance-effective-recruitment-tanya-ridding/.

"When I get a chance, I might look for a technician." Or they wait until they need one. In this business, you can't wait till you need one because then it's too late—you won't be able to take on new jobs that suddenly come your way.

Another problem is that people look for the perfect technician who has the right skills, the right habits, and the right mannerisms to just walk in the door. And take it from me, that's not going to happen.

Our technicians on the front lines are the face of our company—they're the initial gatekeepers for Peterman Brothers—and the recruiting department influences whom those technicians are. The hiring manager has the final say on whom they hire, but our recruiters serve as strategic business partners who give their opinion on which candidate is a perfect fit for a given job.

Peterman Principle

To be a great leader, start by leading the person in the mirror.

There's a lot of competition for talent, and often, the way we compete isn't at the salary negotiation table. It's all the things we do outside of that. It's the culture we create within the company that, hopefully, leads someone to think, "This place is unlike anything I've ever seen before and I want to be a part of it."

Recruiting Makes an Impact

Here's the kind of impact recruitment can have on an organization: At the beginning of 2022, Peterman Brothers had three hundred employees; at the beginning of 2023, we had six hundred. In an industry where the common refrain is that you can't find great people, our recruitment team managed to find three hundred of them.

There are two reasons why that happened: first, our team simply recruited harder, and second, we have the kind of culture that makes people want to join our company.

When I say, "recruiting harder," I'm talking about the amount of time and effort we devote to finding skilled labor. Before we had a recruiting department, I started every one of my days on Indeed, Craigslist, and LinkedIn, trying to connect with great people. One morning I realized this activity shouldn't be our seventh or eighth priority in the day—it should be our first. That's when we launched our own recruiting department.

When I talk with business owners, I tell them if their company is doing $5 million and they want to get to $10 million, hire a recruiter right now. You say you can't afford one? Yes, you can. If a recruiter finds a good technician, that equates to new income for your business—that recruiter will pay for themselves with the first two employees they bring in.

Peterman Principle

Lean into being uncomfortable—growth is just beyond the pain.

How Our Team Works

Our recruitment team consists of a talent acquisition manager who oversees four recruiters. You might envision all our recruiters as bubbly, outgoing sales types, but according to Kurt Conner, our director of human resources, that's not true, and for good reason:

"Our recruiters are a mixed bag of personalities, and that's intentional. We have some outgoing people, and some are very reserved—both types are chosen to match the types of positions they oversee. The main thing they share is that both are very passionate about the Peterman Brothers brand."

In many companies, recruiters are responsible only for doing interviews and hiring people; ours perform a full cycle of activities that let new employees know we value them from the time they receive a job offer.

Kurt explains:

When we realize we have an opening to fill, the recruiter meets with the manager to understand the scope of work and build a job description. Next, the recruiter posts the job to cast a wide net for a diverse candidate pool. From there, they do phone screening, set up interviews, sit in on in-person interviews and guide managers to think about whether someone is truly a good fit for the position.

Along the way, our recruiters also handle personality assessments and skills assessments. When a job offer is created, they extend the offer to the candidate and work with them through the entire onboarding process. Our recruiters also conduct thirty-day, sixty-day, and ninety-day surveys to find out how the new person is doing and whether we need to make changes. Because our recruiters are full-cycle, the person we hire has a friendly, helpful face to accompany them through their first days with Peterman Brothers.

Recruiters at Peterman Brothers can be more strategic than those at many other companies. They influence our overall talent acquisition strategy: they suggest improvements to the process; they teach hiring managers how to improve their interviewing techniques; they do benchmarking based on our competitors; and they check our external branding to make sure our messaging is on target.

Caylie Yoder, corporate recruiter at Peterman Brothers, adds: "We work closely with hiring managers to identify the skills, experience and personal qualities they need for open positions. Good communications with those managers is vital because it lets us get their feedback from interviews faster and keeps the process moving forward."

When we hire a recruiter, we look for someone who has a positive attitude and can adapt quickly to change. With a growing company like ours, if we see that something isn't working in our recruiting strategy, we change it the next day. Our recruiters have to be able to pivot and move quickly in the new direction.

Peterman Principle

The best leaders tell themselves the truth, and they want others to do the same.

Over the past few years, we've plunged into data analytics. We've built a "turnover dashboard" that lets us monitor employee turnover in real time. Our recruiters reach out to new hires every thirty, sixty, and ninety days and ask them about their experience at Peterman Brothers. We track that data and use it to make improvements in the recruitment process.

It's All about Culture

At the end of the day, when a job seeker has three offers, they're going to compare them and consider this question: Which company has the best culture—where would I like to work the most? So everything our recruiters do, from creating an engaging job posting to putting colorful content on our website, has to help our culture stand out from other companies.

Our recruiters are our cultural champions. Any HVAC company can offer someone a job as a plumber, but in the long run, the kind of company offering the job makes all the difference. We count on our recruiters to sell people on the true fact that Peterman Brothers is going to be different. It's a whole new world, something they've never seen before.

Next, I'll talk about how sharing business best practices—with your employees and your competition as well—brings great benefits. It's important to know, however, which information you should share and which you should keep to yourself.

CHAPTER 8

SHARING EMPOWERS EVERYONE

Back in 2018, Tyler and I were overseeing construction of our new building—Dad provided wise counsel along the way—and we had more questions than answers. We needed some new ideas for getting the place done and done exactly right.

I reached out to a mentor of mine, John Conway, an executive at Nexstar, and asked him to recommend someone who could help us. He suggested that I contact Jonathan Bancroft, who ran the HVAC company Morris Jenkins in Charlotte, North Carolina, and ask him for assistance. I called Jonathan, and it was one of the most important and beneficial phone calls I ever made.

When we spoke, he gave me a few ideas for making sure the new building fit our business needs to maximize efficiency. I was taken aback by how open he was—right off the bat, he shared a lot about how his business ran.

As we ended the call, I couldn't resist the urge to ask, "Would you mind if me, my brother Tyler and my dad came down to your headquarters and spent a day with you? I have the feeling that would help us tremendously, not only in constructing our building the right way, but for learning more about how you run your business. I've heard many good things about your operation."

He was hesitant. "Chad, I don't typically give people tours of our building, mainly because I get so many requests for that, and also, it can be a distraction for our employees."

My heart sank. I had the feeling that not only would seeing the facilities at Jon's company help us make our building exactly what we needed it to be, but I also thought that a long-term relationship with Jon would benefit us both.

"I completely understand," I said. "No problem at all. I hope we'll talk again soon."

I'm not sure why, but suddenly he changed his mind. "I'll tell you what, Chad, if you, Tyler and your dad can get down here to North Carolina in two weeks, I'll be happy to show you around. Go ahead and make the arrangements and I'll see you then."

After thanking Jonathan over and over, I told Tyler and Dad the good news about the upcoming meeting. I bought plane tickets for the three of us (the most I had ever spent on airfare) and wasted no time in preparing for the meeting.

Peterman Principle

You will beat out 90 percent of the crowd simply by showing up every day.

When we met with Jonathan, he was very kind. He spent the entire day with us, talking with us as we toured his facilities, which were five times bigger than ours. He introduced us to everyone on his team and graciously answered our questions about creating our building: "We've struggled with this—can you suggest a way to fix it?" "How can we keep costs down?" "Is there a way to do this project faster?"

His advice was immensely helpful, and spending that time with him showed us what is possible for a business in our industry. That has motivated us when times were tough. We knew from his example that there's a way to make our company as big and successful as his; we just have to keep figuring out how to do it.

Just as important, we learned from his sharing. He was selfless in sharing information with us, and he didn't have to be—he chose to do it. As we left him at the end of that day, I thanked him and told him how the information he gave us would be incredibly helpful.

"I'm happy to share, Chad," he said. "There's enough work out there for all of us, so there's no need to be possessive about what we know. Sharing helps others in our industry, which helps the industry thrive, and chances are, people will return the favor and share their knowledge with you as well."

These days, every time I conduct a tour of our facilities for people from other companies, I always think of Jonathan and the great thing he did for us all those years ago.

Sharing Is Essential

There are so many reasons why sharing information—internally and externally—is absolutely essential for building a culture of continuous learning and empowerment. Sharing insights or data can help team members improve their performance and establish a culture of collaboration.

Not only can sharing help to uncover opportunities for growth that otherwise might have gone unnoticed, but it can also help teams spot potential risks or threats to the business that may be lurking in the background.

Peterman Principle

Leaders are there to remove obstacles so that
their team can achieve their goals.

Here are some other important points about sharing information:

- *A "Single Version of the Truth"* – The same accurate, reliable information should flow across all levels of a business. Whether it's good news or bad, it's essential that everyone in the company has the same data in real time. This keeps everyone—no matter where they work in an organization—on the same page.

- *Transparency Leads to Trust* – When employees in a company realize that leaders are being open and honest with them about business matters—even difficult ones—they trust them and are more willing to "buy into" the company mission.

- *Faster Decision-Making* – Employees who are empowered with solid business information feel equipped to make important decisions faster, which can help keep business processes moving at a brisk pace.

- *Many Experts Contribute* – When a variety of employees—inside a company and outside it—are well-informed by shared information, experts in many specialties contribute creative ideas for solving problems, which helps to solve them faster.

- *True Sense of Community* – In many organizations, important business communications are sent only to the "higher ups," but when employees *at all levels* get the same information, everyone realizes they're an important part of the company.

Another reason that we share so much is there's a bigger game out there—helping everybody in the industry get better. Just as an incoming tide raises all ships, if we can help make other companies better, it lifts our whole industry to a higher level, our customers have higher expectations, and everybody wins.

Touring the Facilities

One day every month, we conduct a tour of our entire headquarters for ten to twelve other companies in our industry. We spend the whole day, from 8:00 a.m. to 4:00 p.m., with representatives from those companies, and we share everything and anything they want to know about, things we've figured out or things we think they should consider.

On a typical tour, I spend the first two hours giving the group—mostly business owners, operations managers, and service line managers—an overview of our company's history and our growth, and then I open things up for a Q&A so that people can ask any questions they like.

After that, we go on a tour of our entire 80,000-square-foot headquarters building, which takes about an hour. We go into each and every department, and they see the entire operation. I make it clear that nothing is off-limits.

After lunch, I bring in some of our subject matter experts—usually, managers in our departments such as the call center, marketing, recruiting, and training. We also discuss mergers and acquisitions.

Most often, the comments I get from people after they take the tour is that it's good to see what is possible if people work very hard. They see that we didn't come up with a magic potion—we went through all the steps and overcame all the difficult challenges that they're encountering.

What I always try to reinforce is that they need to take whatever they learned on the tour and go implement it, and put it into play right away. Don't talk about it on the ride back to your company and say, "That would be a great idea." Go do it!

Relying on Outside Sources

Today in my role, I talk to more people outside of the company than I do inside. The biggest reason for that is I always want to get new ideas.

Often, if we're struggling with a problem, our team will come to me and ask, "Here's what we're having a problem with. Can you reach out to your network and see if anybody has figured this out yet? And can we talk to them?"

Luckily for me, the trades industry as a whole is very good at sharing.

Any time somebody outside the company calls me and says, "Can you send over the document you created on how you interview people for jobs?" I say, "Yes, absolutely. Here it is. Take it, use it, plagiarize it, do whatever you want. Hopefully it will help your business."

The companies that are very successful are always willing to share. They're always doing whatever they can to help others. And ultimately, that's why they succeed.

Peterman Principle

There is no problem that can't be solved.

There Are Limits

It's important to know, however, that to protect an organization's interests, there are limits to the types of information that should be shared. Our director of continuous improvement, Deb Albacete, explains:

A company's leaders must establish the boundaries of communications. We believe in being transparent, but some information may have legal or ethical constraints that require caution about sharing—ignoring those boundaries could have serious legal or business consequences. Examples of this include attorney-client privilege, non-disclosure agreements, business contracts and proprietary information. Protecting these boundaries while still providing effective communication reduces risk to your organization and builds the trust of those you are partnered with.

When we share information with others, we grow our influence as leaders. We want to lead from a place of help and support, removing roadblocks for people.

When our team sees me leading people around our building on tours, my hope is that it shows them sharing information is a very good thing. We always say that our mission is to revolutionize the industry one way or another. Sharing is one of the steps we take to make that happen.

In the final chapter, I point out roadblocks to empowering employees, things that leaders do—often, they're not even aware they're doing them—that prevent learning and growth from happening for their team and, ultimately, for their entire business.

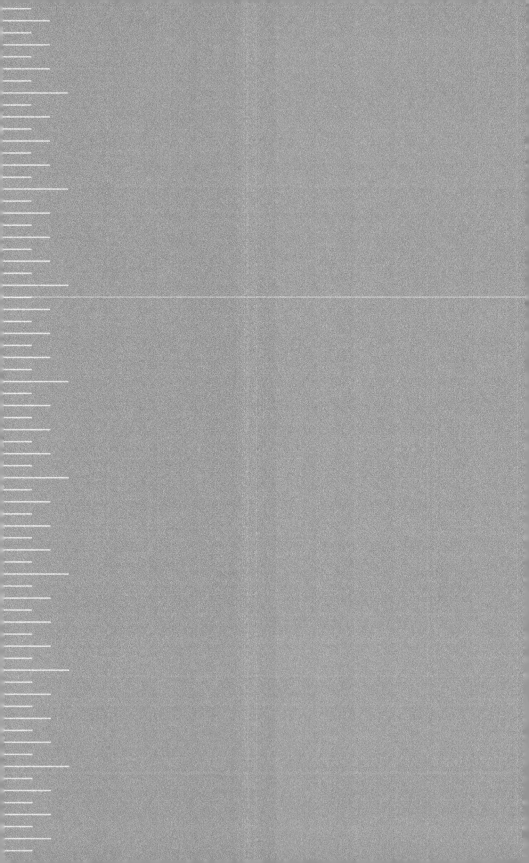

CHAPTER 9

FIVE ROADBLOCKS TO EMPOWERMENT

No matter how much time and effort a company puts into its empowerment project, there will always be roadblocks lurking, threatening to derail the best intentions. Even with the constant focus we put into empowerment at Peterman Brothers, we've learned that we have to be vigilant about keeping these roadblocks from damaging our culture:

Roadblock to Empowerment #1: Lack of Trust

Trust is the foundation of empowerment. If leaders don't trust their team or their team doesn't trust them, it's very difficult to empower people by delegating tasks.

It's important to develop trust within your teams so that employees know the company has their best interest at heart—they're here to support them and help them grow.

Often in our industry, when technicians take on leadership roles, they've done their trade for so long that it's hard for them to comprehend anyone doing the job in a way they wouldn't.

In that case, a leader is going to struggle to offload some responsibilities because they think, "No one does this as well as I do." Obviously, that's not a good way to empower a team.

I have an advantage in this area. Since I've never worked as a technician out in the field, I don't have "my way of doing things." My trust in my technicians is mainly built on the fact that I don't know how to do the work that they do!

To empower employees, a leader has to be aware that people might do things differently. A leader's job is to empower their team by supporting them as they come up with new, creative ways of doing things. Honestly, it's OK if someone does something differently from you.

Trust isn't something in which a leader just tells someone, "I trust you to do the job well." A leader shows trust by their actions, letting someone do a task independently and not trying to guide them every step of the way.

Peterman Principle

Tough situations are always going to come your way—it's how you respond that counts.

Roadblock to Empowerment #2: Fear of Failure

A paralyzing roadblock to empowerment is the fear of failure. This can exist within an entire company, a specific department, or a leader. It's illustrated by a culture that doesn't tolerate mistakes.

In this type of environment, employees are hesitant to do anything because if they fail, there are bad consequences. They're left thinking, "What if this doesn't go well?" "What if my idea doesn't work?" "Will making a mistake cost me my job?"

In this type of culture, a company will struggle to make any movement forward. Recently, I wrote an email to our entire company saying that a lot of success is found in our failures, so we've got to be able to embrace them as opposed to fearing them.

When things are going well and everybody's happy, you can probably look back and say that we didn't learn a lot during that time.

It's when things don't go as planned or you have a rough quarter that people can really dig in, come up with personal strength they didn't know they had, and work on getting better during those difficult times.

When you have a culture that contains fear of failure, no one ever admits they're wrong. Ultimately, you've got a bunch of people not trying to find the right solution but trying to make sure they're not wrong: "No, it wasn't my fault. I didn't do it."

A team is never going to solve a problem if they keep blaming everybody else because they're too scared to say, "Hey, my idea didn't go as planned—I ask for your help in fixing it." No problem ever gets solved until someone takes ownership for it. If we constantly blame one another, we're not solving the problem, but we're just trying to be the one who is right.

Roadblock to Empowerment #3: Inadequate Communication

To empower people, there must be effective communication—leaders who can't communicate clearly or transparently create confusion within their team. We work on this constantly at Peterman Brothers— communication must be effective from executive leadership down to field leadership, who communicate down to field supervisors, who communicate to technicians.

We have to make sure everyone is on the same page by communicating the same key messages. A big problem in the trades is we can't call an "all hands on deck" meeting because all the technicians are out in the field. We have to make sure we communicate clearly to them during office meetings so that they know the things they should focus on.

If you're not getting the business results you want, the odds are it's because of a breakdown in communication. Someone at some level is confused about what they should be doing. That's OK; it's going to happen, but the problem needs to be fixed quickly.

One of the things we work on very hard at Peterman Brothers is career pathing, which lets a technician out in the field know the skills they need to move to the next level. When we started sketching out the core things that people need to do, their focus and commitment jumped to a higher level.

Now people have clear paths that tell them, for example, if they want to become a higher-level technician, they need to work on these five things, and when they master those things, they can move up.

If an employee is having problems, communicate. Go talk to them. If they're not doing what they should be doing, have a conversation: "Let's talk. Let's work together to figure this out." It's a leader's job to let them know the things they should be doing, that they have the resources they need, and that they will be trusted and their ideas will be valued.

Peterman Principle

For a business, growth is happiness.

Roadblock to Empowerment #4: Ego and Insecurity

Leaders who have big egos can feel threatened by talented team members, and because of that, they're reluctant to delegate authority or share credit for success. This causes a roadblock to empowerment because that person always has to be right; they have to be the one who comes up with the big idea.

For a culture of empowerment, it's essential that there is no ego at the top. If you're leading the organization, the more credit you can deflect to your people, the better for everyone.

Chances are that a great leader will receive some awards, which are satisfying, but those awards also present a fantastic time to praise their team, knowing that they're the ones who actually did the work that put the leader in a position to receive those accolades.

A key to a leader "retraining" themselves is showing gratitude, letting people on their team know they're grateful to have them, grateful for their contribution; and grateful for their hard work. The more gratitude a leader shows to others, the less they will feel the need to praise themselves.

Roadblock to Empowerment #5: Not Being Present

For a leader to create empowerment in their team, there's an important guideline—be present. That doesn't mean always being in the office;

it means when you see a team member, ask them how their weekend was. Check in to see if their kid won their baseball game. Ask them how they enjoyed their vacation.

Let them understand that the company cares about them—they're not just a number or a technician doing the job so that we can collect the money. They're important to us.

If we ever have a bad week or a bad month, I know it's time for me to get closer to my team, not further away.

Recently I sat in on a technicians' meeting at 7:00 a.m. and I addressed the group: "Guys, I just want you to know that we love what you're doing out there. Last month may have been tough, but we're going to all band together and make next month the best month of the year."

It's times like that when I need to be present. It would have been perfectly fine for me not to attend that meeting; it's not one that I typically attend. But attending that meeting reinforces our culture that lets people know, "If you're having a bad month, I'm having a bad month. If you need help, I'm going to get it to you."

I don't work from home because I want to be at the office. I want to see my people; I want to talk to them; I want to be around them.

Many times, when leaders from other companies tour our facilities, they say they wish they had a culture like ours. I always tell them there was a time when our company wasn't like this—we've worked on it for years—and a lot of that culture stems from my brother Tyler and I just being present.

Being with our employees all the time—not as their bosses but as their co-workers—is an illustration of something I've always believed in: it's essential to flatten out the organizational chart because at the end of the day, we all need one another.

When it comes to building empowerment, you can't have anybody that is "over you." You can't have a boss. My job may be different from yours, but that doesn't make me more important than you.

If we're all here to empower one another and support one another, there's no organizational chart for that. Everybody's in this together to make it work.

It might have been that my brother and I were introduced to the idea of empowering employees back in 1986, when my dad started his business and encouraged us to value our ideas—no matter how far-fetched—and feel free to act on them.

As Tyler and I grew Peterman Brothers, we saw over and over again the positive effects of empowering our people, so we embarked on our ongoing "empowerment project"—a project that will never end.

Giving our team members the authority to make their own decisions, letting them know they shouldn't be afraid to make mistakes—they're really just opportunities for improvement—and showing that we value them by providing training and a defined career path not only revamp their careers but also change their personal lives for the better.

Yes, we're running a successful home services business, but we've always considered our real business to be changing people's lives.

People who work in the kind of empowering, supportive culture that we provide—and that we strongly encourage all leaders to provide—agree with the final Peterman Principle because they know that it's true:

Peterman Principle

There is no such thing as failure.